CLASSIC PROPLINERS

MAC
0-21004

Classic Propliners

Colin Addison

Airlife
England

ACKNOWLEDGEMENTS

Aero Union (Chico);
ARDCO Aviation (Tucson);
Basler Corporation (Oshkosh);
Broward County Aviation Dept (Fort Lauderdale);
Dade County Aviation Dept (Miami);
Fred Gillie (West Palm Beach);
Lee County Mosquito Control (Lehigh Acres);
Leeds Bradford Airport Authority;
Save-A-Connie Group (Kansas City).

Without the help and enthusiasm of these individuals and organisations the task of preparing this book would not have been possible.

First published in 1992 by
Airlife Publishing Ltd.

ISBN 1-85310-206-7

Printed in Singapore by Kyodo Printing PTE Ltd.

Airlife Publishing Ltd.

101 Longden Road, Shrewsbury SY3 9EB, England.

INTRODUCTION

Classic Propliners is a pictorial tribute to transport aircraft fast disappearing from major airports around the world. Dwindling numbers of piston-engined aircraft have been seconded to less glamorous roles away from the public gaze, often operating from remote locations. Early turbo-prop airliners are also making way for modern technology jetliners with most major carriers and the sight of such types often stirs a feeling of nostalgia from onlookers.

As numbers dwindle, the interest in such types has increased and today enthusiasts are known to travel thousands of miles to visit the few remaining havens of these transport greats. No other aspect of civilian aviation captures the hypnotic mix of sights, sounds and smells found at these locations.

Economics dictate the continued use of many of these aircraft in such diverse tasks as cargo hauling, fire-fighting or bug spraying. Low capital expenditure more than compensates for the constant attention needed to keep often temperamental powerplants in prime working order.

All the illustrations in this book were taken by the author over the last decade.

Below: Pontiac, Michigan is a mecca for enthusiasts of the DC-3 with two operators, Corporate Express and Century Airlines both operating large numbers of the type. The nearby Ford Motor Company plant at Detroit has provided both operators with work transporting motor spares to many distribution centres. Both aircraft in this view are operated by Corporate Express, the aircraft in the foreground still wears the basic U.S. Navy livery which it wore during service at Barrow, Alaska.

Opposite: To celebrate the fiftieth anniversary of Northwest Airlines, Air Atlantique painted one of their Douglas DC-3s in period Northwest livery for airshow and promotional appearances. After the celebrations the basic colour scheme was retained for some considerable time although Air Atlantique titles were applied in preference to those of Northwest.

Below: Douglas C-47A Dakota N66HL rolled off the production line in 1943 and has seen a long career including distinguished corporate service with both Sears Roebuck and the Singer Corporation. Today, the aircraft has been fully refurbished by Orlando-based RWH Aviation who have fitted an executive interior which would stand comparison with the most prestigious executive jet. RWH Aviation exhibited 'Six Six Hotel Lima' at the EAA Sun 'n' Fun fly-in at Lakeland in April 1989 where it attracted a great deal of interest. Interior design features include colour co-ordinated grey trimmings and a cocktail bar.

Atlantique

Below: Air Atlantique have had a long association with the Dakota. Today, most of their fleet have been converted to carry out the task of oil dispersant sprayers although a single example, registered G-AMRA, has been retained in convertible passenger/cargo configuration for freight charters or pleasure flying work.

Opposite: Little expense is spared by the growing number of preservation groups operating old airliner types. The group who own DC-3 N25673 resplendent in Continental Airlines livery are no exception. The aircraft was purchased from Provincetown Boston Airlines after the demise of that airline in the late eighties and following restoration has now appeared on the U.S. airshow circuit aided by volunteer workers and funds obtained from the sale of memorabilia and pleasure flights. The crew of the aircraft wear full Continental uniforms of the time and the aircraft holds a full FAA air transport category licence.

CONTINENTAL
AIRLINES

Opposite: The feeling of passengers aboard N25673 is no doubt reflected by the 'Cloud Nine' slogan on the passing hangar!

Below: Larry Ray of Tucson, Arizona restored DC-3 NC16070 in United Airlines livery over a lengthy period in the 1980s. Unfortunately due to mounting costs Larry decided to sell the aircraft during 1990 when it fell under the auctioneer's hammer at the Santa Monica Aircraft Auction. Today, the aircraft has joined the growing fleet of warbirds and classics with Evergreen Enterprises at Pinal Air Park, Marana, Arizona.

Continental
CONTINENTAL AIRLINES

Opposite: Basler's production line is housed in two adjoining purpose-built hangars at Wittman Regional Airport, Oshkosh. The facility is capable of housing up to ten airframes in a spacious working environment. Engineers are shown making adjustments to a powerplant on an aircraft destined for the air force of El Salvador.

Below: The Basler Corporation of Oshkosh, Wisconsin are proving that the venerable DC-3 will never die. Basler have entered a programme to completely modify, refurbish and re-engine old airframes with turboprops and fit modern avionics. Warren Basler purchases redundant DC-3s from around the world and after the full treatment they sell for around $2,000,000 US. Aircraft retired from military service are preferred as flight log documentation is usually maintained to exacting standards. The redesigned aircraft feature a fuselage stretch forward of the wing which moves the cockpit some 40 inches. The lengthening of the fuselage compensates for the forward weight of the long turbine engines. Most of the test flying programme is carried out at Van Nuys, California where much better year round weather and the locally based FAA examination centre help to speed up the certification process. Shown getting airborne for an airtest is Basler Turbo-67 Dakota N8059P originally manufactured in 1944 and starting a new lease of life 46 years later!

Below: Provincetown Boston Airlines were amongst the few operators still flying the DC-3 on scheduled passenger services during the late '80s. Around that time the company were taken over by the Texas Air Corporation when the fleet were resprayed in the colours of Eastern Express, the commuter division of Eastern Airlines. Despite being very popular with travellers, the DC-3 didn't fit into the modern day image of Eastern and the type was retired with services continuing using Beech 99s and Saab 340s of Bar Harbor Airlines. In early 1989 most of the retired fleet were in storage at Marco Island in Florida awaiting their fate. Fortunately, the DC-3 is still proving to be a valuable asset to smaller operators with limited resources and two aircraft were sold in Mexico for commercial services, with several others going to private operators. When the P.B.A. fleet were retired almost all the aircraft had been repainted in full Eastern livery although one example still carrying the P.B.A. banner was N43PB.

Opposite: The unusual elongated nose profile on DC-3 N25641 houses weather radar equipment, a luxury not afforded to many Dakota crews. This particular aircraft was sold by Basler to a private operator in Florida during early 1989.

BASLER AIRLINES
N387T
BASLER AIR
N918F

Opposite: As well as DC-3 refurbishment the Basler Corporation's airline division operate their own fleet of DC-3s on lucrative contract freight work for a number of the major U.S. small package forwarders including United Parcels and Federal Express. Amongst the fleet is USAC Turbo Express DC-3 N300BF powered by Pratt & Whitney PT6A-67R powerplants.

Below: Eastern Express N130PB escaped the indignity of being hidden in a deserted corner of Marco Island airfield along with the rest of its family and is shown on the main ramp outside the terminal building.

LINES

Opposite: Florida Airmotive based at Lantana near West Palm Beach have operated a number of DC-3s on ad hoc charter work including N165LG which is no longer in service. The company operates a diverse selection of types including examples of the Beech 18 and Britten Norman Trislander.

Below: Familiar to visitors at many U.S. airshows are the Helio Courier aircraft of Jungle Aviation & Radio Service whose aircraft are often used as parachute mounts when not being employed on missionary flying duties. During 1990, J.A.A.R.S. added 1943-vintage C-47A-DL N7043N to their fleet of smaller aircraft, having purchased it from Air Grand Canyon.

N165LG

Below and opposite: Before and after shots of Douglas DC-3 N200MF owned by Missionary Flights of West Palm Beach International. The green and gold livery was a legacy of earlier corporate service. During early 1989 the aircraft appeared in smart new orange and brown colours for Bible supply flights to the underprivileged.

Opposite: 'Hand of Death' symbolism portrayed on the rear bulkhead artwork aboard Zephyrhills-based DC-3 N87745 used exclusively as a parachute mount by the club who claim to be the biggest in the world. During vacation periods as many as four DC-3s are drafted into Zephyrhills for mass parachute drops.

Below: Exterior shot of the same DC-3, the relatively smart paintwork belies the extremely sparse interior of this old workhorse.

CHECK YOUR GEAR
BEFORE YOU JUMP!

Opposite: A large number of privately owned C-47s wear period military markings, including N227GB owned by the Confederate Air Force shown about to depart from Kenosha in Wisconsin.

Below: Douglas re-manufactured one hundred C-47J transports for operation by the U.S. Navy with the designation C-117D. The programme involved the introduction of new wings and tail assembly, modified landing gear and more powerful Wright R-1820-80 engines. The C-117D was dubbed 'Super Dak' and several examples survive in operational service today. This particular example registered N851M is operated by Lee County Mosquito Control at Lehigh Acres, Florida as a support ship.

2L

Opposite: Eagle Wings of St. Lucia titles appeared on DC-3 N10004 at Opa Locka, Miami during 1990 when the aircraft was seen in storage with a similarly marked Beech 18.

Below left: The C-47 was used for landing aid calibration by the Italian Air Force until quite recently. One example, MM61893 operated by 14 Stormo visited the U.K. for the 50th birthday celebration of the type held at Fairford in Gloucestershire.

Below right: The sole surviving Dakota in British military service is ZA947 operated by the Royal Aircraft Establishment in their famous 'raspberry ripple' livery. The aircraft still earns its keep in everyday R.A.E. service and is a regular at U.K. airshows.

Mr Brian
WINGS ST.
N255D

Opposite: The unmistakable nose profile of Super Constellation N6937C sporting the name 'Star of America' — it probably is!

Below: Dakota N62CC made a rare public appearance at Lakeland, Florida in April 1988 for the annual Sun 'n' Fun fly-in.

STAR OF AMERICA
SAC

Opposite: Perhaps the most popular and famous propliner of all time is the Lockheed Constellation. Today, few airworthy examples survive, with just a handful in commercial service as freighters and a pair of restored aircraft with private preservation groups. The Kansas City-based 'Save-A-Connie' group recently completed the mammoth task of restoring L-1049H N6937C to its former glory. Most of the volunteer work force are ex-T.W.A. staff who have donated thousands of hours to see this magnificent aircraft restored to its former glory. 'Three Seven Charlie' was one of only 53 model 1049H's built and was delivered to Slick Airways in 1959. In 1965 it was sold to Airlift International and following service with a number of obscure freight carriers became a bug sprayer in Canada during the mid-70s. During 1975 it made a precautionary landing at Phoenix, Arizona having suffered an engine failure. Shortly afterwards it flew to Mesa where it remained until 1986 when it was purchased by the 'Save-A-Connie' group who descended on the aircraft to carry out the laborious task of making the aircraft airworthy for a ferry flight to Kansas City. Spare parts for the project were obtained from a former Pennsylvania A.N.G. C-121 in storage at Davis Monthan and today the aircraft is attracting much warranted attention on the U.S. airshow circuit. The aircraft is shown landing at Oshkosh after performing in the 1990 show.

SAC
SAC
37C

Below: The flight deck of the Super Constellation showing the flight engineer's position to advantage. The engineer has the difficult task of monitoring engine functions and often has to juggle with fine adjustments to the temperamental Wright R-3350 engines to keep them running in harmony.

Opposite: The VC-121A is powered by Wright R-3350 radials, perhaps the most daunting aspect of the whole restoration programme.

Opposite: The oldest surviving L-049 is N90831 which was restored by T.W.A. staff and donated to the Pima County Air Museum.

Below: A typical Arizona landscape greets visitors to Ryan Field. The ex-Conifair L-749 Constellation provides a welcome shelter from the blistering sun for the local rattlesnake population.

STAR OF
SWITZERLAND
ETOILE DE SUISSE
TWA
B17G

Opposite: The Dominican Republic provides a haven for the last remaining Constellations in commercial service. Both AMSA and AeroChago being operators of the type for freight flights around the Caribbean and to Miami. One example staged through Opa Locka during delivery to Santa Domingo and is shown receiving attention to the nose area. Opa Locka was for many years a stronghold for piston-engined airliners including the Douglas DC-6 in this shot.

Below: Pima County Air Museum situated adjacent to the Davis Monthan storage facility houses a large number of ex-military transport aircraft including this ex-U.S. Air Force C-121 30548.

Opposite: Framed by a Douglas DC-6 of Aerial Transit, the Aerochago L-1049 is unloaded after another regular freight flight from Santa Domingo to Miami International.

Below: 'Connie' start-ups are never less than exciting with clouds of smoke being the order of the day. Previously in storage in Arizona, this aircraft ex-U.S. Air Force 54-4062, was added to Aerochago's fleet in 1990.

HI-583
AVJET

Opposite: The Douglas DC-6 has survived in substantial numbers and today many aircraft still earn their keep flying freight both for reputable and sometimes dubious carriers. Haiti Air Freight had one such aircraft in service during 1990 registered HH-SCA.

Below: Super Constellation N469C has been derelict at Sebring, Florida for many years and the ravages of time are evident in this shot. Plans to remove the aircraft to the Avon Park missile range have come to nothing. The fate of this aircraft is now uncertain but will no doubt be the breaker's torch.

CLASSIC PROPLINERS

Air Atlantique

LINES

N165LG

2L

STAR OF AMERICA
SAC

SAC
SAC

STAR OF
SWITZERLAND
ETOILE DE SUISSE
TWA

Below and opposite: Aerial Transit, formerly known as Bellomy Lawson operate a large fleet of well maintained DC-6s from their facility at Miami. Most aircraft in the fleet wear this attractive green and yellow livery.

98
ANSIT
N98BL

Below: During the late '80s this pristine Douglas C-54 N97810 of Hispaniola Airways operated regular freight flights between Santa Domingo and Miami. Like so many freight operators in the region Hispaniola lasted for only a short time and the whereabouts of the aircraft are unknown.

Opposite: The distinctive nose profile of the heavy Douglas propliners is evident in this shot of a DC-6 undergoing maintenance alongside a Martin 4-0-4 at Miami International.

Below: Detroit's Willow Run Airport was for many years considered to be the Miami of the midwest U.S.A. with large numbers of piston-engined airliners operating freight charters flying automotive spares on behalf of Ford or Chrysler. Today, Willow Run is very much in decline although several operators are still based there including Universal Airlines. During 1990 DC-6 N861TA was added to their fleet and a smart modern green and blue livery was seen for the first time making a refreshing change to the often dowdy schemes seen on similar aircraft.

Opposite: Pratt & Whitney R-2800 air-cooled radial engines power the Douglas DC-6. Stocks of spares for these units are plentiful ensuring the survival of the type into the next century.

Opposite: Trans Continental's fleet of DC-6s, DC-8s and Convairs all wear this attractive yellow, black and white livery.

Below: Antarctic Air have registered offices in Delaware and operate a single DC-6 N41840 from Miami.

Trans Continental
86C
ZANTOP

Opposite: Rich International were another operator of the DC-6 until the cheap DC-8s flooded the market.

Below: Lineas Aereas del Caribe operated a pair of DC-6s from their base at Barranquilla, Colombia until the late '80s. Like so many operators L.A.C. have replaced these venerable old transports with DC-8s which have swamped the second-hand airliner market since their retirement from service with major carriers.

RICH INTERNATIONAL

Below left: The Atlas Aircraft Corporation of Miami were highly respected traders of second-hand propliners during the '80s. In 1986 the company completed refurbishment of DC-6 N104DH which had previously seen service operating out of Hawaii.

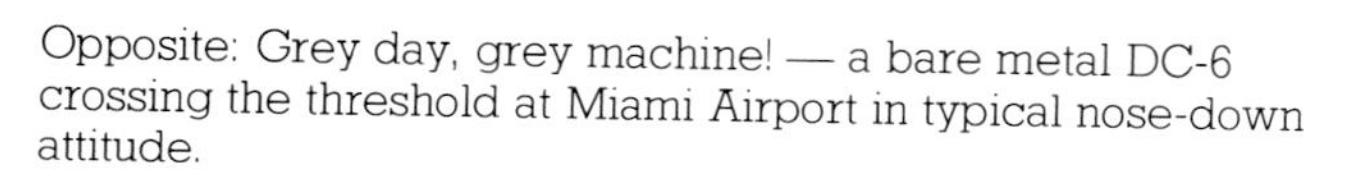

Opposite: Grey day, grey machine! — a bare metal DC-6 crossing the threshold at Miami Airport in typical nose-down attitude.

Below right: Transportes Aereos del Caribe (TAC) operated DC-6 N26BA from the northwest corner of Miami International during 1988.

Opposite: Derelict Douglas DC-6s seen parked in a corner of Fort Lauderdale/Hollywood International Airport during 1987.

Below: Pacific Air Express were a freight operator based in Hawaii. The company fleet included a pair of ATL 98 Carvairs and DC-4 Skymaster N301JT seen stored in potentially airworthy condition at Chandler Memorial Airpark, Arizona during July 1990.

Opposite: Great Southern Airways C-54D N90201 ventured across the Atlantic from the USA to Europe during the late 1980s to uplift a cargo of explosives. During the visit the aircraft made a brief visit to Prestwick to collect fuel. Today the aircraft is still in service and was seen receiving attention at Naples, Florida in April 1989.

Below left: Deceased DC-6, Convair and Beech 18 await the scrap merchant at Fort Lauderdale.

Below right: Few airworthy DC-7s survive although the number was increased by one when N372WG arrived at Miami during the summer of 1990 after many years stored in Panama as HP-847. The arrival at Miami was not without incident as two of the main wheel tyres blew on landing revealing even more of the already visible canvas!

DANGER →
PELLER
AVIATION

Opposite: The Vickers Viscount first flew in 1948 and was the world's first turbo-prop transport. Today dwindling numbers remain airworthy with just a handful of commercial operators. In the U.K., British Midland operated the type until the late '80s before final retirement in favour of Douglas DC-9s. During the latter stages of service with B.M.A. one aircraft registered G-AZNA was painted in the now familiar 'Diamond' livery.

Below: Evolved from the military Canadair CL-44-6 (Yukon) side-loading transport the CL-44D-4 was the first swing-tail commercial transport to attain production. Only 27 aircraft were built, these aircraft closely resembling the Bristol Britannia from which they were derived. The Eire-based cargo airline Aer Turas operated this example when photographed at sunrise on a visit to Leeds Bradford Airport. Today Aer Turas operate a fleet comprised exclusively of DC-8 jetliners.

British Midland BM
NA

Below: British Air Ferries of Southend operate several Viscounts in both passenger and cargo configurations. Over the last decade B.A.F. aircraft have sported a variety of colour schemes, the company appearing unable to decide on a definitive image. Viscount 802 G-AOHM is illustrated during a period when full B.A.F. titles were dropped in favour of the proclamation 'British'.

Opposite: Old and new together — a B.M.A. Viscount is framed by a Douglas DC-9. Some of the DC-9s in the fleet are themselves getting long in the tooth, this particular example being built in 1966.

BMA
BRITISH MIDLAND
BMA

Opposite: B.A.F. have converted two of their fleet to the freight role with a large cargo door on the port side of the fuselage. One example being series 808C G-BBDK shown wearing 'Freightmaster' titles.

Below: Virgin Atlantic have leased several different Viscounts from B.A.F. including G-AOYP shown at Leeds Bradford Airport whilst operating a passenger charter.

Freightmaster
LEEDS & BRADFORD AIRPORT
LEEDS & BRADFORD AIRPORT
HYSTER
HYSTER

Below: Originally designed to meet an American Airlines specification, the Lockheed L-188 Electra was first flown in 1957. A total of 172 Electras were built including N861U which was photographed in 1986 at Orlando, Florida following the collapse of Trans International.

Opposite: Largest operator of the Viscount outside the U.K. is Jadepoint U.S.A. who formerly traded as Go-Air. Most of the aircraft in the fleet are early Srs.700 machines fitted out for V.I.P. or executive flying. Over the years the Viscounts have been used by numerous rock bands during major tours of the U.S.A. The fortunes of the company now seem to be in decline as the call for such work falls to the attraction of more modern equipment. One example in the fleet is N460RC shown several years ago — today the same aircraft sits inactive at Tucson.

N460RC
GO Viscount

Opposite: Derived from the Electra, the P-3 Orion is a maritime reconnaissance variant of the original civilian airliner. The aircraft serves in many of the world's major forces including the Dutch Kon. Marine.

Below: Lockheed L-188AF HR-TNT is operated in the freight role by T.A.N. of Honduras, the aircraft being a converted L-188A originally manufactured in 1959.

RESCUE
300

Below: Mexican registered L-188 Electra XC-HEB turned up in Florida during 1988 when it was photographed awaiting overhaul in the northwest corner of the airport.

Opposite: The Hawker Siddeley (formerly Avro) 748 first flew in 1960 with production continuing well into the '80s with aircraft being built both in the U.K. and under licence in India. During 1990 Aberdeen Airways were operating a pair of aircraft leased from Dan-Air.

Aberdeen Airways

Opposite: Even in the 1990s, the old propliner is an invaluable asset to operators specialising in the aerial application of fire retardants, oil dispersants and pesticides. The fact that such types are used is basically down to economics; where low unit costs are essential to viable operation. However, the availability of more surplus piston-engined cargo types is fast diminishing and operators are having to look elsewhere for replacements. Fortunately, early turbo-prop types such as the Lockheed C-130A and P-3A Orion are coming onto the secondhand market having been replaced by updated variants in military service. Many of the major aerial application companies in the USA are turning to these turbo-prop types to expand fleets, although the old piston aircraft will doubtless survive for some years to come. One of the largest operators of fire bombers is Aero Union of Chico in Northern California who operate a mixed fleet of C-54s, P-2 Neptunes and P-3 Orions. All the aircraft in the fleet wear a high visibility red, white and black livery.

Below: In the USA Fairchild manufactured the F.27 under a licence agreement with Fokker. The type proved highly successful both in the commercial airliner field and as an executive transport with corporate operators.

01
N4989P
03

Opposite: Built in 1958 for the U.S. Navy 'Tanker Zero Three' is a P2V-7 Neptune operated by Aero Union. The Douglas C-54Q in the background was built in 1945 and today both still carry out vital fire suppression duties.

Below: Aero Union lost Douglas C-54B N67109 in an accident during a training sortie at Chico in the spring of 1990. The undercarriage collapsed during circuit work but fortunately the crew all survived the ensuing fire.

03
AERIAL

Opposite: T.B.M. Aviation of Sequoia, California have chosen the Lockheed C-130A Hercules as a replacement for the C-54. During a visit to Sequoia in early 1990 T.B.M. staff were busy preparing the fleet for the coming season.

Below: When this photograph was taken Aero Union's entire fleet of Douglas C-54s was up for sale pending the introduction of the P-3 Orion.

64
64

Opposite: Another company evaluating the C-130A during 1990 were Hemet Valley Flying Services based at Hemet/Ryan, California.

Below: High visibility patches and large tanker code markings have been applied to this C-130A still wearing basic U.S. Air Force camouflage.

Below: C.D.F. Trackers originally wore a green and orange livery which has now been replaced by a high visibility red and white colour scheme. Marsh Aviation of Mesa, Arizona are engaged in a programme to convert the S-2 using TPE.331 turboprops.

Opposite: Hemet Valley Flying Services operate a large fleet of ex-U.S. Navy Grumman S-2 Trackers on behalf of the Californian Department of Forestry including N446DF shown undergoing maintenance at Hemet/Ryan.

94
CDF
94

Opposite: Fairchild C-119 Flying Boxcar N13744 is unlikely to be seen again in the aerial firefighting role. The type proved inadequate for the task and Hemet Valley Flying Service retired their four aircraft in favour of other types.

Below: Operators of fire bombers have to compete for lucrative contracts from the Californian Department of Forestry every year and the quiet winter season is spent preparing aircraft for inspection. Douglas C-54 N460WA of ARDCO was selected for detachment to Hemet for the 1990 season.

Below: Tucson is a regular haunt for propliner fans where the sight of old aircraft, along with the smell of avgas and spent oil provide a hypnotic atmosphere. This active C-54 shares the ramp with an assortment of airworthy and semi-derelict types.

Opposite: Fire bombers can be found in the most unlikely places — these two Douglas C-54s were found on a desert strip at Pacoche, Arizona along with a third example.

RESTRICTED
150

Opposite: Nobody works for fire bomber operators expecting to work in modern facilities. Most maintenance is carried out in the open air often relying on equipment as old as the aircraft themselves. Here a sick powerplant is removed from an ARDCO C-54.

Below: Whatever happened to clean white overalls! — the Harley Davidson sweat shirt is an indication of this particular engineer's recreational interest.

2FY-854

Below: T & G Aviation of Chandler Memorial Airpark are the world's largest operator of the Douglas DC-7. Contract work regularly sees these aircraft detached as far away as Alaska or Africa.

Opposite: Central Air Services of Tucson operate a large fleet of C-54s including 'Tanker 148' shown sat out in the brush at Avra Valley whilst on detachment.

148
N67062

Opposite: Lockheed Harpoons saw civilian service with a number of spraying contractors although all those used in the firefighting role have now been withdrawn.

Below: T.B.M. Aviation donated Fairchild C-123 Provider N3142D to the Pima County Air Museum following retirement from active duty.

112
N7251C

Opposite: Lee County Mosquito Control operates a fleet of Douglas DC-3s on spraying duties waging war against Florida's annual plague of these disease carrying insects. Public opinion has dictated that the aircraft are used only in severe situations where application of pesticides from ground vehicles proves inadequate. If the aircraft are called upon, flights are usually carried out at first light often in formations of up to three aircraft. The control unit operates from private restricted facilities at Lehigh Acres airstrip where both ground and air forces are based. Previous U.S. Air Force and U.S. Army colour schemes are evident on this line up of aircraft.

Below: Environmental Air Services (EASI) of Belle Glade, Central Florida operate several DC-3s in a smart green and orange livery on spraying contract work.

Opposite: The Martin 4-0-4 was derived from the earlier model 2-0-2 featuring more powerful engines, pressurization and extended fuselage. Only 101 examples were built for airline service and few survive today. Marco Airways operated the type on scheduled services around Florida.

Below: Provincetown Boston Airlines operated the Martin 4-0-4 alongside DC-3 and NAMC YS-11 turboprops. Following the demise of P.B.A. this example remained in storage in Naples.

Marco Airways

Below left: Martin 4-0-4 N40436 formed part of the scenery on the Hill Air ramp at Fort Lauderdale for a number of years. Plans to sell the aircraft to a Venezuelan operator failed when extensive corrosion was discovered during a main spar inspection. The aircraft was subsequently broken up and the remains sold to a scrap dealer.

Opposite: Vortex International Martin 4-0-4 N149S was still active during early 1989 when the aircraft was seen at Miami International. The Curtiss C-46 in the background made news headlines in the U.S.A. when it fell to the ground in northern Florida following the failure of a winch cable on a Skycrane helicopter whilst the C-46 fuselage was being transported from Miami to a test range.

Below right: Smart gold and white C-47B N834M is used as a back-up aircraft by Lee County Mosquito Control.

Opposite: Systems International were still operating the Martin 4-0-4 in 1990 from their base at Bartow, Florida. As with so many operators work for these old machines is sparse and two aircraft were seen stored at Fort Lauderdale in 1989.

Below: Another inmate at Hamilton Aviation was this Convair 440 of Omega Airlines.

SYSTEMS- INTERNATIONAL A
N145S
259

Below: Convair flew their first pre-war commercial transport in 1947 designated the CV-240. The aircraft survives today in large numbers in a number of variants ranging from the early V-240s to updated model 440s and turboprop 580/640 series machines. Renown Airlines operate a mixed fleet of Convair variants including 440 N202RA captured at Sarasota, Florida where the airline took up temporary accommodation during 1988.

Opposite: Martin 4-0-4 N3711K was in storage at Chino near Los Angeles when photographed. Despite its immaculate appearance the aircraft had not flown for some considerable time.

N3711K

Opposite: Long term residents in a corner at Opa Locka during the '80s were Super Constellation N1007C and Convair 240 N240BN. The latter was the prototype model 240, but despite the historical significance of the aircraft it was broken-up for scrap along with the Constellation. Dade County Aviation Department who run the airfield, sold both during efforts to smarten up the airfield in order to attract lucrative executive business. Today, Opa Locka has changed dramatically and few propliners are to be seen any more.

Below: Canada West Air Convair 640 C-GCWY was seen in storage on the Hamilton Aviation ramp at Tucson during 1990.

Opposite: Sierra Pacific operate a fleet of Convair 580s from Marana, Arizona. Less fortunate were the fleet of Convairs in the background retired by American Eagle and stored at Marana awaiting sale.

Below: Trans Florida Airlines operate several Convair variants from their base at Daytona Beach including model 240 N1022C.

SIERRA
PACIFIC
N73153

Opposite: The last registered owner of Convair 440 N912AL was the Broward County Sheriff's Department following seizure for smuggling.

Below: Air Resorts Airlines operate Convair 580s on scheduled passenger flights out of San Diego, California. Charter work involves flying Japanese tourists to the Grand Canyon during vacations in the U.S.A.

N912AL

Below and opposite: Only a handful of the 3,234 Junkers JU-52s originally produced remain active today. One example is owned by the German flag carrier Lufthansa. During 1990 the aircraft was engaged on a promotional tour of the U.S.A. visiting major cities throughout the country. The aircraft is flown by Lufthansa crews who normally fly Boeing 747s and Airbus aircraft. The Junkers was one of the highlights at the 1990 EAA fly-in at Oshkosh.

Below: Ford Trimotor N7584 is still active with a full FAA air transport category licence. Visitors to many airshows in North America have the opportunity to take a pleasure flight in this aircraft.

Opposite: Stinson's SM.6000 Trimotor first appeared in 1930 as a cheap alternative to other trimotor types available at the time. Several examples still survive including this aircraft painted in period American Airlines livery.

U.S. MAIL
A.M. 8
Flagship
TEXAS
United Air Lines

Opposite: Propliner fans readily accept aircraft as small as the Grumman Widgeon as many have operated over the years for commercial operators. Lycoming powered N1AS is privately owned and was photographed on Lake Parker, Lakeland, Florida.

Below: Grumman's large HU-16 Albatross has become popular with preservation groups throughout the U.S.A. Most aircraft appear in military markings and are part of the warbird scene. One exception is N8523H operated by the Flying Boat Club from Opa Locka, Florida.

Opposite: The Grumman G-21 Goose in the foreground of this classic line-up at Fort Lauderdale was restored after a long period of inactivity at Fort Lauderdale.

Below left: Hill Air restored Grumman Mallard N42DA to its former glory at Fort Lauderdale.

Below right: Still earning a living is Grumman Widgeon N945JD shown in the colourful livery of Lucaya Air.

Opposite: The unique Bird Innovator — a four-engined conversion of a PBY Catalina. Improved performance was attained with the addition of two Lycoming engines. Purchased during the '80s by an owner in Titusville, Florida the aircraft remained grounded for a number of years due to a legal wrangle. It was suggested that the additional engines had been fitted so that the aircraft could be used in clandestine smuggling operations. The owner successfully cleared his reputation but the aircraft remained grounded at Tico in 1990.

Below: No examples of the Boeing 377 Stratocruiser survive today although several ex-military C-97s are airworthy surviving as freighters or fire bombers. One example registered N8540D was impounded at Fort Lauderdale for drug smuggling during the late '80s when this photograph was taken.

267-0086

Below: De Havilland Canada produced the DHC.4 Caribou to meet a U.S. Army/Canadian Armed Forces specification and the first aircraft flew in 1958. Principal operator of the type was the U.S. Army who ordered 164 aircraft. Powered by Pratt & Whitney R-2000 powerplants the type is still seen in limited numbers. Illustrated is a U.S. Army Caribou visiting Tamiami in July 1990.

Opposite: Amongst the exhibits at Pima County Air Museum are a pair of Boeing C-97s. In the foreground is a former Balair machine used during the Biafran airlift which carries Swiss civilian marks HB-ILY. The aircraft in the background is a KC-97 flight refuelling variant.

BA
U.S. AIR FORCE
0151

Opposite: Douglas produced 243 C-124 Globemaster transports for the U.S. Air Force. The type powered by four Pratt & Whitney R-4360 engines was capable of carrying 200 troops. The huge size of the aircraft is shown to advantage in this shot of an aircraft preserved at Pima County.

Below: Boeing's 307 Stratoliner was built as a pressurized 33-seater with only two prototypes and eight production aircraft being manufactured. Pima County Air Museum were fortunate to secure the preservation of one aircraft formerly registered N19903.

MAC
0-21004
U.S. AIR FORCE
130361

Opposite: Over 3,000 Curtiss C-46 transports were built during the Second World War. Today, only a handful survive in operational use mainly in Alaska, South America and Canada. One example registered N611Z was operated by Florida Aircraft Leasing until quite recently. Following retirement the company donated the aircraft to the Pensacola Naval Air Museum.

Below left: Surplus Lockheed 18s became popular as corporate transports during the 1960s & '70s. Several companies offered modification programmes to update the type with plush executive interiors and refinements. A number of aircraft including N6711 were converted to nose wheel configuration, whilst another example registered N896JB retained the tailwheel.

Below right: Lockheed produced their model 12 as a smaller six-seat version of their model 10 Electra. One example painted in Frontier Aviation colours is amongst a fairly substantial number of present day survivors.

N611Z

Opposite: First flown in 1950, the De Havilland DH.114 Heron was a successful transport in both the civilian and military role. The Royal Navy finally withdrew their remaining aircraft in 1989 when they were replaced as station 'hacks' by Jetstream aircraft.

Below: Pima County Air Museum maintain a Curtiss C-46 in U.S.A.A.F. colours.

NAVAL AIR COMMAND
ROYAL NAVY

Below: Handley Page produced the Dart Herald to contend in the market dominated by the Fokker F.27 and Avro 748. The type never gained the acclaim of its brethren and few aircraft survive today. Before the demise of Euroair the company operated several Heralds including G-BEYK.

Opposite: Another view of the Starflite facility showing C-46 N625CL in the foreground with a former Royal Canadian Air Force C-47 to the rear.

Opposite: A rare photo opportunity at Naples during 1988 when the stored Carvair was seen in company with a Douglas C-54 from which the type was derived.

Below: The Bristol 170 Mk.31 was designed from the outset as a military freighter, although the type was never adopted by the R.A.F. A total of 214 aircraft were built including G-BISU which was the last of the type to see commercial service in the U.K. with Instone Airlines.

F

Below: AESA of El Salvador operated a number of different Douglas DC-6s during the 1980s. Miami International was a regular haunt for these aircraft which operated from the northwest corner of the airport away from the jet cargo centre seen as a backdrop to this atmospheric evening shot as the DC-6 trundles across to its dispersal area.